DISCOVER LANDS
Beautiful
Yorkshire

John Potter

MYRIAD
LONDON

West Yorkshire

West Yorkshire is a landscape of contrasts. There are great differences between the physical landscapes of the west and centre where the Pennines reach a height of 1,725ft (526m) and are cut into by the valleys of the Wharfe, Aire and Calder and their tributaries that made the region such a fulcrum of growth and change during the Industrial Revolution, to the relatively low-lying eastern lowlands on the edge of the Vale of York. There are contrasts, too, in the urban landscapes of the great cities of Leeds and Bradford, the major towns of Halifax, Huddersfield and Wakefield, and the small towns such as Keighley, Pontefract and Wetherby. But all is not urban and industrial; there are interesting villages such as Heptonstall and Howarth and great houses such as Harewood House and Temple Newsam.

Leeds

Leeds, the commercial and financial capital of Yorkshire, has many fine buildings. Dominating the heart of the city is Leeds Town Hall, constructed between 1853-58 and designed by Cuthbert Brodrick, the Hull architect. It is topped by a magnificent domed clock tower rising to 225ft (68m). The gilded owl (above), stands beside the Civic Hall (1931-33). A new market hall (above right) was built in 1904 by architects John and Joseph Leeming at the junction of Kirkgate and Vicar Lane, replacing the original market hall of 1857. Today, new building is a hallmark of Leeds. Leeds Waterfront (right) was the city's dockland area at the termini of the Aire and Calder Navigation and the Leeds and Liverpool Canal.

By the 1960s, this area was run-down and derelict. It has now been transformed. Existing warehouses have been converted and new riverside office buildings constructed.

Kirkstall Abbey *right*

The ruins of Kirkstall Abbey lie just three miles north-west of Leeds city centre. This abbey was founded in 1147 by monks and lay brothers from Fountains Abbey but they did not move to Leeds until 1152. It is believed that the church was completed within 25 years. In 1890 the site was bought from a private owner and presented to Leeds Corporation who undertook repairs before opening it as a park in 1893. The romantic ruins have inspired many artists including JMW Turner.

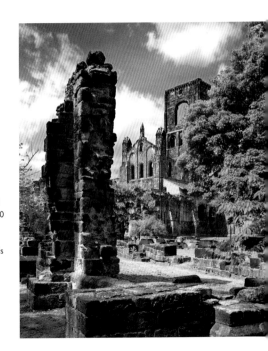

Harewood House *below*

This magnificent country house, the home of Earl and Countess Lascelles, was built by the York architect John Carr between 1759 and 1772 on the instructions of Edwin Lascelles whose father had made his fortune in the ribbon trade, from his position as collector of customs in Barbados and his directorship of the East India Company. The interiors were the work of Robert Adam and much of the furniture is by Thomas Chippendale. In the 1840s the south façade of the house was remodelled by Sir Charles Barry, the architect of the Houses of Parliament. The grounds were laid out by Lancelot "Capability" Brown who dammed Gawthorpe Beck to create a serpentine lake and planted groups of trees on the slopes on either side of the lake. To the south of the house is an ornamental garden with intricate flower-beds, fountains and herbaceous borders. Still the home of the Lascelles family, Harewood House is one of Yorkshire's major tourist attractions.

Bradford *right & below*

Bradford's magnificent neo-Gothic Town Hall dates from 1873; the scale of the building reflects Bradford's prominence and its ambition as a commercial centre of trade, worthy of being ranked with other cities such as Liverpool and Glasgow. Re-named City Hall in 1965, its frontage overlooks Centenary Square and is graced with sculptures of British monarchs, including Oliver Cromwell – an echo of Bradford's role in the Civil War. The Alhambra Theatre was built in 1914 for the musical impresario Frank Laidler, the "King of Pantomime". It was restored in 1986 after suggestions that it might be demolished and a car park built in its place. Two of Bradford's surviving medieval buildings are Bolling Hall and the Cathedral. Now a museum, and just a mile from the city centre, Bolling Hall gives visitors an insight into the lives and times of the two families for whom it provided a home for over five hundred years. During the Civil War the household supported the Royalist cause, and Bolling Hall was a stronghold during the "Siege of Bradford".

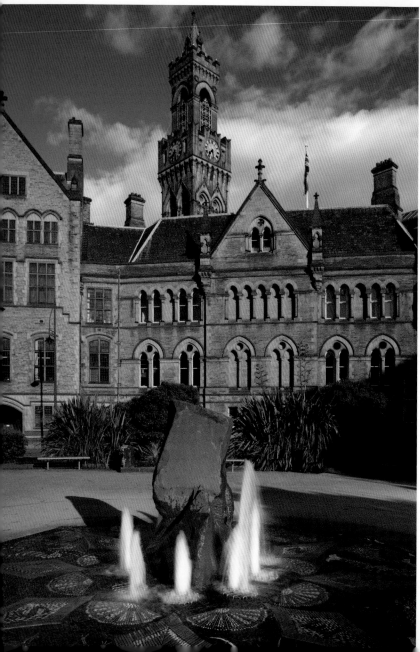

Huddersfield *left & right*

The West Riding town of Huddersfield boasts 1,660 listed buildings – only Westminster and Bristol have more. One of the town's most famous sons was the Labour prime minister Harold Wilson. His statue was erected in 1999 and graces St George's Square in front of the railway station. Built between 1847-48, the station has been called "a stately home with trains in it". Its classical facade is 416ft long and is supported by eight 68ft high columns. The roof of the town's magnificent open-air market is supported by cast-iron pillars, a detail of which is shown above. Huddersfield's magnificent town hall doubles as a concert hall and is home to the town's renowned choral society.

Haworth *above & below*

The photograph below is of the Brontë Parsonage Museum at Haworth; the one above is of the town centre. When the Rev Patrick Brontë brought his family to live at the parsonage in Haworth in 1820 the village was little more than a cluster of stone cottages clinging to a steep hill, with the church at the top of the street and the moors stretching into the distance. Today the fame of the Brontës has spread far and wide and visitors descend on the town in their thousands. The Parsonage is full of paintings, books and papers that belonged to the Brontës and the rooms have been restored to convey what life was like for the parson and his family. The village retains its Victorian air with cobbled streets, an old-fashioned apothecary's shop, booksellers and antique shops. A network of paths radiates from the village into the countryside. Visitors can make their way to the Brontë Falls and Top Withens on the moors above Haworth. The setting of this farmhouse, now in ruins, is thought to have inspired Emily Brontë's *Wuthering Heights*.

Halifax *left & inset below*

In a valley seven miles south-west of Bradford, Halifax is the capital of Calderdale. The town owes its prosperity to the wool trade and its town hall was designed by Sir Charles Barry, the architect of the Houses of Parliament. The Piece Hall (detail below) completed in 1779, contains more than 300 rooms built around an open quadrangle; it was here that handloom weavers living in outlying cottages bought their "pieces" of woollen cloth to sell. The Wainhouse Tower was built for John Edward Wainhouse to carry the smoke and fumes produced by his dye works out of the Calder valley. At 253ft (77m) high it is one of Calderdale's best-loved landmarks.

Other Halifax attractions include the Victoria theatre which dates from 1901 and was originally a concert hall. Converted into a theatre in 1960 it is currently being refurbished. The hands-on Eureka! children's museum opened in 1992 and is located in the railway station.

Holme Valley *left*

The Digley reservoir is one of a number in the upper Holme valley overlooking Holmfirth. Immediately to the west is the smaller Bilberry reservoir which burst its bank in 1852, causing the death of 81 people in the valley below.

Castle Hill *right*

The hill fort at Almondbury near Huddersfield, seen here from Farnley Tyas, is made up of a series of Iron Age and medieval earthworks. The flat topped hill has been the site Chartist rallies as well as prize-fighting. The Victoria or Jubilee tower was added in 1899 to celebrate Queen Victoria's Diamond Jubilee two years earlier.

Heptonstall *above* and Hebden Bridge *right*

The ancient hilltop village of Heptonstall is home to two churches, which both share the same graveyard. The ruined church of St Thomas à Becket dates from 1256 and was dedicated to Becket, the archbishop who was murdered on the orders of the king in 1170 and became a symbol of resistance to authority. In 1847 this medieval chapel was partially destroyed in a great storm. A new church, in the Victorian Gothic style (above) was built. Dedicated to St Thomas the Apostle it was consecrated in 1860 and contains the 11-sided font from the old chapel; its bells too have incorporated those from the ruined church and ring out over the hills and valleys, calling the congregation to prayer. The magnificent view (right) is of Hebden Bridge from Heptonstall. Eight miles west of Halifax, Hebden Bridge grew rapidly in the 18th and 19th centuries as a result of the wool trade, the fast-flowing waters of the river Calder providing power for the mills in the area.

Holmfirth *right & below*

Three miles south of Huddersfield, Holmfirth is situated at the confluence of the rivers Holme and Ribble. This picturesque Pennine town developed rapidly in the 16th century thanks to the burgeoning cloth industry and its local slate and stone mines. Now the town and its surrounding countryside are best-known as the setting for the long-running television series *Last of the Summer Wine*. Thousands of tourists flock to the area each year to enjoy the scenery and hoping to identify locations used in the series. Sid's Café in the centre of the town, a watering hole familiar to all *Last of the Summer Wine* viewers, is now a place of pilgrimage for

fans. Next door to the character Nora Batty's fictional house in the series is the Summer Wine exhibition which combines the Wrinkled Stocking Tea Room and a re-creation of the character Compo's home.

The Dales

The Yorkshire Dales National Park which straddles the Pennines is an area of outstanding natural beauty where pretty villages nestle amidst the typical Dales scenery of drystone walls and barns or close to stark limestone escarpments. The grandeur of the Three Peaks, the scenic Settle to Carlisle railway line and the outstanding limestone scenery of Malhamdale are all to be found in this region.

West Burton *right*

The typical Wensleydale village of West Burton is famous for the West Burton Falls, just east of the village, a popular location for artists and photographers.

Richmond *above*

The capital of Swaledale, Richmond is dominated by its castle keep, part of the massive castle built by Alan the Red of Brittany, a trusted supporter of William I. Richmond ranks among the most beautiful towns in England, with many elegant Georgian houses, cobbled streets and pretty cottage gardens. At the centre of the impressive market place is the 12th century chapel of the Holy Trinity, now used as the regimental museum of the Green Howards. In 1788, Samuel Butler, a local actor and manager, built the Theatre Royal, a small and beautiful Georgian theatre, which is still in use today. Situated in the middle of Richmond at the bottom of the market place and overlooked by Millgate House, a beautiful Georgian townhouse, is a beautiful south-facing walled garden, open to the public between April and October.

East Gill Force
right

The small village of Keld nestles snugly at the head of Swaledale, its pretty stone cottages clustered around a tiny square. The name of the village derives from the old Norse word "keld", meaning spring and the nearby river Swale is fed by many small becks which flow down from the surrounding fells. Ten minutes' stroll from the village, just north of the Pennine Way, where the long-distance footpath crosses East Stonesdale, is East Gill Force.

Gunnerside *above*

The beautiful windswept fells and attractive patchwork of fields, drystone walls and barns along the valley bottom make this part of Swaledale a favourite with visitors. In early summer the wildflower meadows are a vibrant sea of colour, and a delight to walk through. Gunnerside Gill runs through the tiny village of Gunnnerside and meets the river just below the King's Head Inn.

Kisdon Hill *left*

Swaledale is one of the more remote northern dales, to the west of Richmond. The limestone mass of Kisdon Hill stands at the head of Swaledale. This viewpoint looks south towards Muker.

Castle Bolton *left*

Dominated by Bolton Castle, the small village of Castle Bolton
is five miles west of Leyburn. This massive fortress has loomed over
Wensleydale since 1379 and is one of the country's best preserved castle
Mary Queen of Scots was imprisoned here in 1568 and 1569.
In the middle of the village is a wide green and St Oswald's, the attractive
14th century church, nestles in the shadow of the castle.

Aysgarth Falls *below*

Situated seven miles west of Leyburn, Aysgarth is best known for the
spectacular waterfalls on the river Ure that cascade down a series of larg
limestone steps. Riverside walks link the Upper, Middle and Lower Falls
which are all within a mile of each other. The best view of the Upper Fore
is from the 16th century bridge in the centre of the village.

Askrigg *below*

Just one mile north-east of Bainbridge on the northern side of
Wensleydale, Askrigg is a tiny settlement best known as the setting
for the popular television series *All Creatures Great and Small*. Above the
village sits Askrigg Common and beyond it the unmistakable form of
Addlebrough. Askrigg was a former medieval market town and is now
popular with walkers and daytrippers.

Dent *above*

The pretty village of Dent is actually in Cumbria, four miles south-east of Sedbergh, although it lies within the Yorkshire Dales National Park. The white-painted cottages are very Cumbrian in character in contrast to the warm stone buildings usually found in the lower Yorkshire Dales.

Middleham *left*

Situated just two miles from Leyburn between Coverdale and Wensleydale, Middleham is another village dominated by its castle. This impressive defensive structure was built around 1170 by Robert Fitz Randolph during the reign of Henry II. The massive central keep has 12ft (3.5m) thick walls and is one of the largest in England. The countryside around Middleham is famous for the training of racehorses.

Ribblehead Viaduct *below*

The 72-mile Settle-Carlisle railway line is one of the most picturesque in Britain and runs through Ribblesdale offering dramatic views of Whernside and Pen-y-Ghent. Constructed in the 1870s, the line was renovated and reopened in 2000. The magnificent 24-arch Ribblehead Viaduct to the north-west of Ribblehead station is seen here from Runscar Hill.

Malham

The extraordinary limestone landscape of Malhamdale is a great attraction for visitors and walkers. It was formed over millions of years, first as a result of glacial erosion and then by the effects of wind, rain and frost. Three of the best examples – the limestone cliff at Malham Cove, Malham Tarn and Gordale Scar – are sited behind the attractive village of Malham (left). Above the Cove lies Malham pavement (right), where hundreds of limestone blocks or "clints" are indented by deep fissures or "grykes".

Great Whernside *above*

Wharfedale and Nidderdale run parallel to each other in a north-west to south-easterly direction. From Buckden to Bolton Abbey, Wharfedale has magnificent upland scenery. The rugged fell of Great Whernside dominates the skyline east of Buckden. Not to be confused with Whernside (one of the Three Peaks further west) it reaches a height of 2,310ft (705m) and creates an abrupt change from the lush pastures below. The long boulder-strewn ridge gives extensive views across Nidderdale to the east and westward to Wharfedale.

Halton Gill *left*

A village with a spectacular setting, Halton Gill is sheltered by Plover Hill, Cow Close Fell and Horse Head Moor. The stone houses and farm buildings of the village sit beside the infant river Skirfare with its attractive packhorse bridge.

Scalebar Force *right*

In a deep wooded ravine just outside Settle, on the road to Kirkby Malham, Scalebar Force is a cascading waterfall in a deeply wooded valley. During wet weather the pretty rivulet changes into a raging torrent. The word "force", a Yorkshire dialect word for a waterfall, comes from the old Norse word *fors*, which is sometimes corrupted to "foss".

Buckden *above*

The annual Buckden Pike Fell Race starts and finishes on the gala field in Buckden. The event draws runners from across the north of England, and watching them aiming for the top of Buckden Pike (2303ft/702m) is a great spectacle. At the summit is a poignant memorial to the Polish crew of an aircraft that crashed here in 1942. Just one man survived – he made it to safety by following the tracks of a fox in the snow.

Wharfedale *above*

Running from north to south, from the high moors of Langstrothdale to Ilkley, Wharfedale is one of the Dales' longest and most beautiful valleys. The unique and stunning landscape of Wharfedale is revealed in this view from Rowan Tree Crag looking towards Hartlington Hall and Kail Hill, just east of Burnsall.

Burnsall *below*

Ten miles north-west of Ilkley, the picturesque village of Burnsall is famous for the massive five-arched bridge (built on the site of a former packhorse bridge) which spans the meandering river Wharfe. Every August, the village hosts a feast and sports day which includes England's oldest fell race.

Appletreewick *right*

This peaceful Wharfedale village four miles south-east of Grassington rests on a steep slope overlooked by the craggy summit of Simon's Seat. The main street is lined by ornate and characterful cottages with High Hall at the top and Low Hall at the bottom. The original owner of High Hall was Appletreewick's most famous inhabitant, Sir William Craven. Known as "Dick Whittington of the Dales" he was the son of a local farmer who was sent to London to make his fortune and eventually became Lord Mayor of the City in 1610. Loyal to his roots, William returned to Appletreewick and rebuilt High Hall.

Bolton Priory *left*

This beautiful Augustinian priory is a stone's throw from the village of Bolton Bridge five miles west of Skipton. The magnificent ruins are immensely popular with visitors who enjoy picnicking and strolling along the banks of the river Wharfe. Close by, the river gushes in a thunderous cascade though a narrow chasm known as "the Strid". Further upstream, along a nature trail, is Barden Bridge and the beautifully sited Barden Tower, which was built in 1485 by Lord Henry Clifford.

Jervaulx Abbey *below*

Situated between Masham and Leyburn are the ruins of this atmospheric Cistercian abbey. Dating from 1156 the abbey fell into ruin after the Dissolution in 1537. Enough remains of the ivy-covered crumbling walls to remind us of the simple yet austere lives of the "white monks". A weathered effigy of the abbey's great benefactor, Hugh Fitzhugh, stands in the grounds. The site is closely identified with Wensleydale cheese since it is thought that the monks at Jervaulx first perfected the recipe.

Vale of York

This large region of low-lying, undulating countryside stretches from the river Tees in the north to Selby in the south, a distance of more than 50 miles, and from the eastern edge of the Yorkshire Dales in the west to the Howardian Hills and the Yorkshire Wolds in the east. Underlain by glacial deposits it is a rich agricultural area with hay meadows along the river floodplains and large fields elsewhere intensively cultivated for arable crops. There are scattered small woods and larger conifer plantations on sandy soils. The farmhouses and villages are built of a distinctive mottled brick with pantile roofs. The Vale of York is an important transport corridor containing the A1 and A19 trunk roads and the East Coast Main Line railway connecting London with Edinburgh. The region includes the busy market towns of Northallerton, Knaresbrough and Thirsk, the elegant spa town of Harrogate and the cathedral cities of York and Ripon.

York Minster *above*

The largest Gothic cathedral in northern Europe, York Minster is the seat of the archbishop of York, the second highest office in the Church of England. There has been a church here since 627; work on the current Minster began in 1220 and was not completed until 1472. York Minster is famous for the Great East Window, completed in 1408, the largest expanse of medieval stained-glass in the world. Just outside the Minster is a statue of Constantine who was proclaimed Roman emperor in York in AD306.

Lendal Bridge *right*

This elegant iron bridge, with stone towers at either end, was built by Thomas Page in 1863. It is one of nine bridges over the river Ouse in York.

Kilburn White Horse *above right*

Early morning frost covers the fields close to the village of Coxwold in the beautiful Vale of Mowbray. On the distant escarpment is the White Horse of Kilburn. This striking chalk figure in the shape of a horse was carved into a hillside overlooking the Vale of York in 1857 and can be seen from 40 miles away.

Clifford's Tower *above*

This distinctive stone fortification in Tower Street is all that remains of the 13th and 14th century keep of York Castle. In 1190, a mob began to attack the city's Jewish residents and, fearing for their lives, 150 people took refuge in the wooden tower which then occupied this site. The militia laid siege to the tower for several days, when a fire broke out. All the people inside the tower perished in the flames or committed suicide rather than surrender themselves to the mob.

The Shambles *above*

One of York's highlights is the Shambles, a meandering medieval street leading up to the Minster. Today it is filled with souvenir shops; in the Middle Ages it was home to many butchers (the name Shambles comes from the Anglo-Saxon words *shammels* or *fleshshammels* – meaning an open-air slaughterhouse). Most of the buildings along the Shambles are medieval but there are also some outstanding Tudor half-timbered houses.

Knaresborough *right*

The beautiful town of Knaresborough grew up around the steep sides of the gorge of the river Nidd. This has been a strategic point for centuries and during the Middle Ages Knaresborough was firmly established on the royal circuit. The Norman castle was used as a hideout by the four knights who murdered Thomas à Becket in 1170. It was badly damaged during the Civil War when the Parliamentarians besieged the Royalists; a decree in 1646 ordered its destruction and many buildings in the town centre are constructed from "castle stone". The castle's remains are open to the public and its grounds are used as a performance space – in particular for events during the Knaresborough Festival every August. In 1851 the dramatic viaduct across the gorge was completed.

Harrogate *left*

The first mineral spring was discovered at the Tewitt Well in this North Yorkshire town in 1571. By the 18th century, Harrogate had become a fashionable spa to rival Bath and Buxton. The Royal Pump Room has been converted into a museum telling its story. It is possible to visit the sulphur wells where more than 15,000 people would come for treatments. Next to the museum is Valley Gardens where many of the wells were found. Today it is one of the town's beautiful public parks.

Newby Hall *right*

Sir Christopher Wren guided the design of Newby Hall, near Ripon, built in 1697. Since 1748 it has been home to the Compton family whose ancestor, William Weddell, bought the property and enlarged it during the 1760s. The interior was re-modelled by a variety of architects, including Robert Adam, and it is an exceptional example of 18th century interior design. The present grounds were laid out in the 1920s, with herbaceous borders and a dramatic broad grass walk leading down to the river Ure. In 2007 Newby Hall was used for the filming of the television adaptation of Jane Austen's novel *Mansfield Park*.

Thirsk *left*

This lively town lies south of Northallerton overlooking the Hambledon Hills and close to the North York Moors. Thirsk has a long tradition of flower displays and is a frequent award-winner of the Yorkshire in Bloom competitions. The town is built around an impressive medieval market square which hosts a twice-weekly open-air market. The church of St Mary is over 500 years old and the nave has a beautiful timbered roof. One of the stained-glass windows in St Anne's chapel was created from the jumbled fragments of other windows in the church during a major 19th century restoration project. A plaque marks the birthplace of Thomas Lord who founded Lord's cricket ground; his home now houses Thirsk Museum. Thirsk's most famous modern resident was the author James Herriot (the pen name of James Alfred Wight) who practised as a vet at 23 Kirkgate, now home to the World of James Herriot Museum. Herriot's semi-autobiographical stories – known as the *All Creatures Great and Small* novels – tell of the eventful life of a small-town vet living and working on the edge of the North York Moors.

Summer shows

Agricultural shows, large and small, have been the lifeblood of agricultural communities, and great social occasions, throughout the county for generations. The grandest of these is the Great Yorkshire Show held over three days at the showground on the edge of Harrogate. Other notable summer shows are the Malton Show and the Ripley Show, held in the grounds of Ripley Castle. The classic car rallies held at Newby Hall are also great crowd-pullers.

Castle Howard *above*

One of Britain's finest historic houses Castle Howard, 25 miles north-east of York, was built to a design by John Vanbrugh between 1699-1712 and is set amongst magnificent parkland. This opulent residence is, along with Blenheim near Oxford, regarded as a masterpiece of English Baroque architecture. It gained fame with television audiences when it was used as the setting for *Brideshead Revisited*, the 1981 adaptation of Evelyn Waugh's celebrated novel.

North York Moors

One of the finest upland landscapes in Britain, the North York Moors include the north-east corner of Yorkshire stretching northwards from the Vale of Pickering to the border with County Durham and from the Hambleton and Cleveland Hills in the west to the coast. A large part of the region has been designated as a national park. With its heather-clad moorland, fertile dales and characterful villages and market towns, this region has one of Yorkshire's most beautiful and captivating landscapes. Dales penetrate the moorlands; from the North Sea coast, for example, Eskdale runs deep inland and Farndale and Rosedale penetrate northwards from the Vale of Pickering. These dales within the moorlands have always been very important. They have heavy clay soils that are variable in quality, but in such barren surroundings they have a crucial role and contain almost all the village settlements.

Blakey Ridge *right*

The famous Lyke Wake Walk, a long-distance footpath, traverses the east to west watershed of the North York Moors through remote and mostly uninhabited moorland, passing Bronze Age burial mounds and lonely prehistoric standing stones en route.

Roseberry Topping *below*

On the border between the North York Moors and Cleveland, the distinctive half-coned shape of Roseberry Topping dominates much of the countryside around Guisborough. The hill's peculiar shape is due to the fact that half the summit has collapsed, owing to a geological fault or because many old alum or ironstone mines lie close to the top. On nearby Easby Moor there is an impressive monument to Captain Cook who went to school in nearby Great Ayton.

Mallyan Spout *above*

The highest waterfall on the North York Moors, Mallyan Spout, near Goathland cascades 60ft (18m) down the side of West Beck Gorge. A short walk alongside the beck just to the right of the Mallyan Spout Hotel leads to the waterfall. In wet weather, spray is blown across the path giving visitors the impression of walking through a waterfall.

Rosedale *above*

This is a long, extended valley which stretches out in a south-easterly direction from Westerdale Moor and Danby High Moor towards Hartoft End and Cropton Forest. The river Seven flows throughout its length and there are superb views across the dale from the road near the Lion Inn on Blakey Ridge. The Rosedale Show is held every August in the delightful village of Rosedale Abbey. The picturesque church of St Lawrence is at the heart of the village.

Hutton-le-Hole *left*

Home to the Ryedale Folk Museum, this beautiful village is a popular stopping-off point for visitors. Its broad village green, dotted with moorland sheep, is an ideal spot for a summer picnic. The Folk Museum, Yorkshire's leading open-air museum, has historic buildings depicting the past lives of north Yorkshire people.

Rievaulx Abbey *right*

Cistercian abbeys were usually situated in secluded locations; the site of Rievaulx Abbey in the depths of the narrow Rye valley must have provided the monks with a haven of peace and solitude. The ruins of the ancient abbey show that this was once one of the finest monastic churches in northern Britain. Fine views of the abbey can be enjoyed from the Rievaulx Terrace and Temples which are situated on an escarpment high above the valley.

Hole of Horcum *left*

Hollowed out of the heather-clad moor beside the Pickering to Whitby road, the Hole of Horcum is a huge natural amphitheatre. Legend has it that "the devil's punchbowl", as it is known locally, was created by a giant named Wade who scooped out the rocks and earth, tossing them two miles east to Blakey Topping. A popular circular walk from the roadside car park passes this derelict farm cottage at Low Horcum.

Sutton Bank *below*

The Hambleton Escarpment rises abruptly to a height of around 1,000ft (305m), giving views of more than 30 miles. Roulston Scar and Hood Hill lie to the left. Gormire Lake is lit by a dramatic sky stirred up by strong winds sweeping across the Vale of York.

Bridlington *above*

With two glorious long sandy beaches, miles of elegant promenades and a very pretty and bustling harbour Bridlington has all the ingredients for the perfect holiday resort. Flamborough Head and its lighthouse are clearly visible from the north pier and beach. The town is divided into two parts, the old town about a mile inland which originated around the abbey at Bridlington Priory and the holiday resort and fishing port at the quay fringing Bridlington Bay. Bridlington's first hotel was opened in 1805 and it soon became a popular resort for the city-dwellers of West Yorkshire. The Beside the Seaside Exhibition close to the harbour contains fascinating exhibits of the town in its heyday.

Bempton *left*

At the southern end of Filey Bay, Bempton Cliffs were bought by the RSPB in 1969 and it is one of the best known nature reserves for seabirds in the UK. Throughout the year more than a quarter of a million birds nest here. Puffin, guillemot and kittiwake abound on the cliffs and a major attraction is the huge gannet colony – the only nesting site for these birds on the British mainland. Access for visitors is easy by car or on foot from the little village of Bempton, one mile inland. The best time to see the seabirds is during the nesting season from June to August, although visitors can enjoy bracing walks along the cliffs and visit the RSPB visitor centre throughout the year.

Flamborough *right*

The coastline at Flamborough Head is one of the most spectacular areas of chalk cliff in Britain. Dramatic cliffs, some reaching 400ft (122m), thrust up out of the sea, providing a haven for wildlife. Thornwick Bay is just one of the many sheltered, shingle coves fronting the sea with caves and dramatic stacks. The old Beacon lighthouse at Flamborough was first built in 1674. The new lighthouse was built in 1806 by John Matson of Bridlington.

Humber Bridge *above*

Opened in 1981, this beautiful suspension bridge was built to link north Lincolnshire and Humberside across the wide Humber estuary. Almost 1.5 miles long, the bridge has cut 50 miles off the road journey between the major ports of Hull and Grimsby. The south tower of the bridge is founded in shallow water 1,650ft (500m) from the shore.

The Deep *right*

The glass and aluminium marine life centre – called The Deep – was conceived to educate visitors about the worlds' oceans. It stands at the confluence of the rivers Hull and Humber.

Spurn Head *left*

Situated on the north bank of the entrance to the river Humber, this three-mile long finger of land that snakes out into the Humber estuary is constantly being reshaped by storms and coastal erosion. The distinctive black-and-white lighthouse became redundant in 1985 and has now been replaced by automatic beacons.

South Yorkshire

South Yorkshire ranges from high, bleak moorlands in the west, covered in heather and blanket bog, without a sign of habitation, through the densely populated Coal Measure country containing the city of Sheffield and the towns of Barnsley and Rotherham, to the fertile agricultural country of the Magnesian Limestone belt, and then stretches beyond Doncaster to the east to the Humberhead Levels only a few feet above sea level. It is a many-layered landscape created by the endeavours of people using its resources over many thousands of years to make a living and create farmsteads, villages and urban and industrial settlements, large and small. Yet this densely populated region contains many architectural and landscape gems including fine medieval, 18th century and Victorian buildings, public parks and country houses with their surrounding parks and gardens. In the west there are large sweeps of open country and elsewhere tracts of attractive walled, hedged and wooded farmed countryside.

Sheffield *above & below*

The centre of Sheffield is dominated by the Town Hall, built of Derbyshire sandstone, standing at the junction of Surrey Street and Pinstone Street. Designed by EW Mountford, it was described by Sir Nicholas Pevsner as "a large picturesque pile". It was opened by Queen Victoria in 1897, who was greeted by Sheffield's first lord mayor, the Duke of Norfolk. Two friezes carved in stone adorn the exterior walls; they depict, among other things, grinders, smiths, smelters and miners. The 200ft tower (below) is surmounted by an 8ft high bronze statue of Vulcan, the Roman god of fire and furnaces, with his right foot on an anvil and pincers in his left hand. On a sunny day, the Peace Gardens (above) provide a welcome green space for students and office-workers. The distinctive curved roof on the far right is that of the Winter Gardens; opened in 2002, it houses over 150 species of plants.

Bradfield Moors

The physical setting of Sheffield is equalled by no other British city. It is enveloped in the west by very extensive tracts of high moorland and upland pastures (below) rising to more than 1,800ft (550m), all within the modern city boundaries and much of it part of the Peak District National Park. No moorland can be bleaker or more beautiful, according to the season, than the Bradfield Moors which stretch westwards from Bradfield village beyond Agden Reservoir reaching in their highest parts to more than 1,500ft (457m).

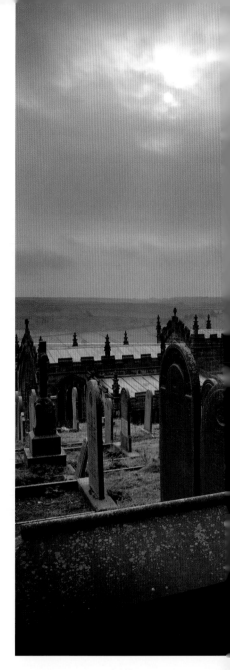

Bradfield church *above*

There are two Bradfield villages, Low Bradfield and High Bradfield. Dominating High Bradfield is St Nicholas' parish church, one of the largest churches in Hallamshire. The churchyard contains some very old gravestones but most interesting is one dating from 1864 when the nearby Dale Dyke Reservoir burst its banks and the rushing torrent of water, pouring down the Loxley valley towards Sheffield, resulted in the death of 240 people. Gravestones in the churchyard include that of James Trickett, his wife and three children who all perished in the flood; the last two lines of the dedication reads: "Whate'er the fault this is most true, The Flood is a warning to me and to you." Also buried here is William Horsfield who first discovered the crack in the embankment but too late to save many of his neighbours. He died in 1881. At the entrance to the churchyard is what is reputed to have been a watch-house, built as a lookout point to discourage body-snatchers who removed fresh corpses from graves to sell to doctors and hospitals for medical study.

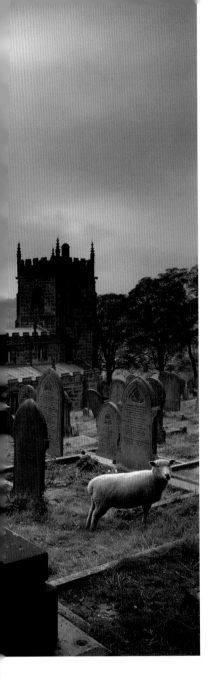

Barnsley Town Hall *above*

Barnsley's Town Hall, sited at the junction of Church Street and Shambles Street at the top of Market Hill, was erected when Barnsley was the coal capital of South Yorkshire and still dominates the townscape today. Constructed in 1932-33, of white limestone blocks, it was designed by the Liverpool architects, Briggs & Thornely. It replaced the dingy old Town Hall in St Mary's Gate. Its imposing frontage, 21 bays long, is surmounted by a conspicuous clock tower. But it may not have ever had a clock tower – it was omitted from the final design on financial grounds and consent by the town council for its construction was only given at the last minute, four months after the foundation stone was laid. The cost of building and furnishing came to £188,000, an enormous figure in the depression days of the 1930s.

Stainborough Castle *left*

Stainborough Castle is a recently renovated mock medieval castle sited in the beautiful gardens of Wentworth Castle. This recently renovated country house is not a castle and not at Wentworth but at Stainborough, near Barnsley. The hall consists of a north-west facing wing built by Sir Gervase Cutler between 1670-72 together with a north-east facing wing in the Baroque style which was finished in the 1720s and a Palladian-style front-facing south-east elevation built between 1759-64. In 1948 the house, outbuildings and 60 acres of garden were bought by Barnsley Education Committee. In 1949 it opened as a teacher training college and in 1978 became Northern College. The grounds of the house hold a Grade 1 listing. It featured in BBC Television's *Restoration* series.

Wentworth Woodhouse *above*

The mansion that can be seen from the park at Wentworth is the East or Palladian front. It was begun by Thomas Watson-Wentworth (later the Marquis of Rockingham) in 1732. It superseded another house facing west built in the florid Baroque style. The Palladian front extends to a length of 606ft (183m), the longest country house front in England. From the village of Wentworth the park is entered beside the Octagon Lodge, one of five surviving lodges. Some visitors entering the park for the first time from this direction are so impressed by the stable block with its clock tower that they think that it is the mansion! The deer park is the only remaining deer park in South Yorkshire that still contains deer. The 100-strong herd can often be glimpsed grazing among the trees that are scattered throughout the park.

Roche Abbey

left

Roche Abbey was founded in 1147 on a site given by two patrons, Richard de Busli and Richard Fitzurgis. It is a typical Cistercian site, tucked away in a secluded spot with a good water supply.

Although only an inner gatehouse and the church transepts reach to any height, a complete Cistercian abbey plan is exposed in the ruins. In the 1770s Capability Brown was employed by the owner, the Earl of Scarborough, to landscape the site and he covered up and planted over the ruins of the abbey. These have now been fully exposed to reveal the full abbey site.

...usworth Hall
...d Park *right*

...illiam Wrightson (1676-1760)
...s the owner responsible for the
...lding of the hall that stands today.
...e Rotherham mason-architect,
...orge Platt, began to supervise the
...lding of the new hall and on his
...ath in 1742 his son, John, took
...er. Later extensions were
...signed by James Paine, the
...ladian-style architect. William
...rightson's son-in-law, John Battie-
...rightson, commissioned Richard
...oods, the landscape gardener, to
...prove the 100 acres of grounds
...rrounding the new hall between
...50-53. Features of the landscaped
...k dating from this period include
...ee lakes, a bridge, a grotto-like
...athouse and a cascade. The park
...d the house now belong to
...ncaster Metropolitan Borough
...uncil, the house having become a
...seum in 1967. The house and
...k underwent restoration
...tween 2004-7 partly funded by a
...9m Heritage Lottery grant.

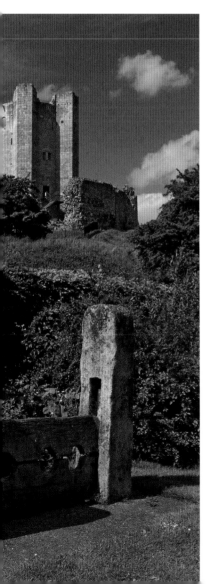

Conisbrough Castle *left*

This magnificent stone castle
stands aloft on a tiny "island" of
Magnesian Limestone, controlling
an important crossing point on the
river Don. Dominating all is the
stone keep, a massive cylindrical
tower, nearly 99ft (30m) high with
walls 15ft (4.6m) thick. Attached to
the basic cylinder shape are six
splayed buttresses which rise to
become turrets. By Elizabethan
times the castle was in disrepair
and was never garrisoned during
the Civil War of the 1640s. This
saved it from destruction. Now the
floors of the keep have been
reinstated and the conical roof is
once more in place.

Brodsworth Hall *above*

South Yorkshire has a rich heritage
of country houses, parks and
gardens. Brodsworth Hall, five
miles north-west of Doncaster, is
a fine Italianate-style country
house, of Magnesian Limestone,
built and furnished between 1861-
63 for Charles Sabine Augustus
Thellusson. The house and
grounds remained in family
ownership until 1990 when they
were acquired by English Heritage.
After a five-year programme of
restoration and conservation they
were opened to the public in
1995. The house was designed by
Chevalier Casentini. As far as is
known Casentini never came to
South Yorkshire and his designs
were executed by a little-known
architect called Philip Wilkinson.
From the entrance hall there is a
magnificent sequence of halls on
the ground floor with painted
marbling on the walls and *scagliola*
(imitation marble) columns and
pilasters. The gardens include a
large formal garden of
symmetrical beds, with stunning
bedding schemes, cut out of the
turf in shapes said to have been
unchanged since they were laid
out in the 1860s. There is also an
Italianate summerhouse.

Fishlake Church *left*

St Cuthbert's, the medieval church in Fishlake, a small village on the flatlands to the north-east of Doncaster, is mainly in the Perpendicular style. It is reputedly dedicated to St Cuthbert because monks carried the remains of St Cuthbert hermit monk, from the Farne Islands around northern Englan for several years to keep them out of the hands of the Viking raiders, and Fishlake is supposed to be one of the places where his remains rested for a period. The south doorway of the church, all that remains of the Norma church that once stood on the site, is probably the most lavishly carved medieval church doorway in Yorkshire.

Sprotbrough Church *far left*

The oldest parts of St Mary's, Sprotbrough, date from the late 13th century. The solid tower was heightened in the Perpendicular period when William Fitzwilliam, who died in 1474, left £40 for the work. There are fine brasses to William and his wife on the chancel floor. The church has stone effigie of a late 13th century knight, a 14th century lady and of Philip Copley (who died in 1577) and his wife. There is also "a mysterious stone seat", the so-called "Frith Stool" with 14th century carvings.

Tickhill *left & below*

Tickhill is perhaps the most pleasant small town in South Yorkshire. The centre of the town has the air of an ancient market town unaffected by industrialisation. This atmosphere enhanced by the fact that the town centre has two rookeries and the churchyard is carpeted with celandines in early spring The town is dominated by St Mary's parish church, one of the most oustanding Perpendicular churches in south Yorkshire. This stately building contains magnificent stone tombs, coffins, an iron-bound wooden chest and medieval stained-glass.

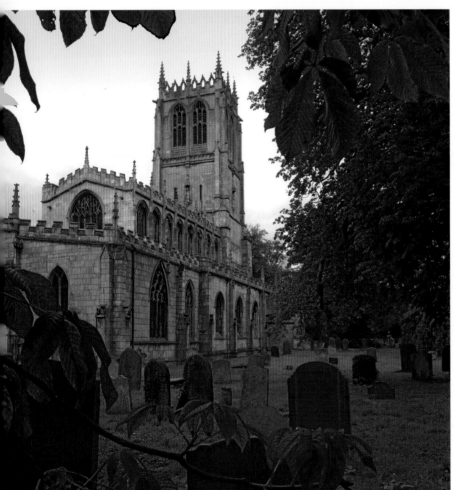

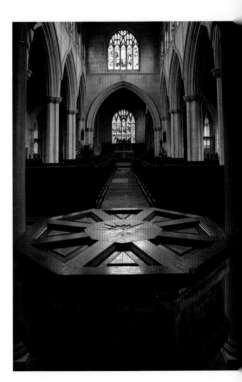

First published in 2010
by Myriad Books Limited,
35 Bishopsthorpe Road, London SE26 4PA

Photographs copyright © John Potter
Text copyright © John Potter

Consultant editor Melvyn Jones

ISBN 1 84746 358 4
EAN 978 1 84746 358 6

Designed by Jerry Goldie Graphic Design

Printed in China

www.myriadbooks.com